Zero Trust Security

Edgewise Special Edition

by Lawrence C. Miller and Katherine Teitler

for dummies®
A Wiley Brand

Zero Trust Security For Dummies®, Edgewise Special Edition

Published by
John Wiley & Sons, Inc.
111 River St.
Hoboken, NJ 07030-5774
www.wiley.com

Copyright © 2018 by John Wiley & Sons, Inc.

No part of this publication may be reproduced, stored in a retrieval system or transmitted in any form or by any means, electronic, mechanical, photocopying, recording, scanning or otherwise, except as permitted under Sections 107 or 108 of the 1976 United States Copyright Act, without the prior written permission of the Publisher. Requests to the Publisher for permission should be addressed to the Permissions Department, John Wiley & Sons, Inc., 111 River Street, Hoboken, NJ 07030, (201) 748-6011, fax (201) 748-6008, or online at http://www.wiley.com/go/permissions.

Trademarks: Wiley, For Dummies, the Dummies Man logo, The Dummies Way, Dummies.com, Making Everything Easier, and related trade dress are trademarks or registered trademarks of John Wiley & Sons, Inc. and/or its affiliates in the United States and other countries, and may not be used without written permission. Edgewise and the Edgewise logo are registered trademarks of Edgewise. All other trademarks are the property of their respective owners. John Wiley & Sons, Inc., is not associated with any product or vendor mentioned in this book.

LIMIT OF LIABILITY/DISCLAIMER OF WARRANTY: THE PUBLISHER AND THE AUTHOR MAKE NO REPRESENTATIONS OR WARRANTIES WITH RESPECT TO THE ACCURACY OR COMPLETENESS OF THE CONTENTS OF THIS WORK AND SPECIFICALLY DISCLAIM ALL WARRANTIES, INCLUDING WITHOUT LIMITATION WARRANTIES OF FITNESS FOR A PARTICULAR PURPOSE. NO WARRANTY MAY BE CREATED OR EXTENDED BY SALES OR PROMOTIONAL MATERIALS. THE ADVICE AND STRATEGIES CONTAINED HEREIN MAY NOT BE SUITABLE FOR EVERY SITUATION. THIS WORK IS SOLD WITH THE UNDERSTANDING THAT THE PUBLISHER IS NOT ENGAGED IN RENDERING LEGAL, ACCOUNTING, OR OTHER PROFESSIONAL SERVICES. IF PROFESSIONAL ASSISTANCE IS REQUIRED, THE SERVICES OF A COMPETENT PROFESSIONAL PERSON SHOULD BE SOUGHT. NEITHER THE PUBLISHER NOR THE AUTHOR SHALL BE LIABLE FOR DAMAGES ARISING HEREFROM. THE FACT THAT AN ORGANIZATION OR WEBSITE IS REFERRED TO IN THIS WORK AS A CITATION AND/OR A POTENTIAL SOURCE OF FURTHER INFORMATION DOES NOT MEAN THAT THE AUTHOR OR THE PUBLISHER ENDORSES THE INFORMATION THE ORGANIZATION OR WEBSITE MAY PROVIDE OR RECOMMENDATIONS IT MAY MAKE. FURTHER, READERS SHOULD BE AWARE THAT INTERNET WEBSITES LISTED IN THIS WORK MAY HAVE CHANGED OR DISAPPEARED BETWEEN WHEN THIS WORK WAS WRITTEN AND WHEN IT IS READ.

For general information on our other products and services, or how to create a custom *For Dummies* book for your business or organization, please contact our Business Development Department in the U.S. at 877-409-4177, contact info@dummies.biz, or visit www.dummies.com/biz.html. For information about licensing the *For Dummies* brand for products or services, contact BrandedRights&Licenses@Wiley.com.

ISBN: 978-1-119-54270-4 (pbk); ISBN: 978-1-119-54282-7 (ebk)

Manufactured in the United States of America

C10004127_082918

Publisher's Acknowledgments

Some of the people who helped bring this book to market include the following:

Project Editor: Carrie A. Burchfield
Editorial Manager: Rev Mengle
Acquisitions Editor: Ashley Barth
Business Development Representative: Sue Blessing

Table of Contents

INTRODUCTION 1
    About This Book 1
    Foolish Assumptions 1
    Icons Used in This Book 2
    Beyond the Book 2

CHAPTER 1: The Basics of Zero Trust Security 3
    Recognizing the Limitations of Traditional Network Security 3
    Bringing Protection Closer to the Application Workload 5
    Reducing Risk in Cloud-based and Dynamic Architectures 7

CHAPTER 2: Implementing an Inside-Out Methodology 9
    Understanding the Methodology 9
    Mapping Your Attack Surface 10
    Preventing Lateral Movement by Attackers 11
    Implementing Least Privilege 13
    Creating Application Workload Centric Policies
    for Cloud Agility 13

CHAPTER 3: Verifying Application Workload Identities 15
    Understanding and Visualizing Risk 15
    Fingerprinting Workloads 16
        Unchanging characteristics 16
        Understandable characteristics 17
        A broad variety of characteristics 17
        Upgrade tolerant 18
    Verifying Identity 18

CHAPTER 4: Getting Started with Zero Trust Security 21
    Step 1: Identify Your Assets 21
    Step 2: Analyze Your Data Flows 22
    Step 3: Protect Strategic Assets 22
    Step 4: Monitor and Adapt 23

CHAPTER 5: The Business Benefits of Zero Trust Security 25
   Reduce Risk by Identifying Assets and Improving Visibility 25
   Gain Greater Control in Your Cloud Environment 26
   Achieve Lower Breach Potential 26
   Aid Compliance Audit Initiatives 27
   Increase Business Speed and Agility 27
   Alleviate Organizational Friction 28

Introduction

With enterprise networks increasingly operating in both on-premises data center and cloud environments, security teams must find new ways to protect application workloads and prevent data breaches without disrupting business operations. Traditional network security controls, such as firewalls deployed at the perimeter, are outmoded. Any security controls that assume the veracity of data, applications, or communications inside a "trusted" network are inadequate to manage and protect today's workloads. The core tenet of zero trust security is "never trust, always verify." Although zero trust isn't a new security concept, it's not easy or practical to implement in a complex enterprise network unless you use the right methodology and technology.

About This Book

In this book, you discover how to successfully implement zero trust security to protect your business. *Zero Trust Security For Dummies*, Edgewise Special Edition, consists of five chapters that explore the following:

- » What zero trust security is all about (Chapter 1)
- » How to implement a zero trust security methodology (Chapter 2)
- » How to visualize, fingerprint, and identify application workloads (Chapter 3)
- » How to get started with zero trust security (Chapter 4)
- » Six business benefits of zero trust security (Chapter 5)

Foolish Assumptions

It's been said that most assumptions have outlived their uselessness, but we assume a few things nonetheless. Mainly, we assume that you're a security practitioner, such as a chief information security officer (CISO) or a cloud or network architect, a security operations or DevOps professional, or a network engineer. Therefore, we assume that you have at least some security and networking knowledge. This book is written primarily for technical security practitioners who are looking to gain more knowledge about zero trust security.

If any of these assumptions describe you, then this book is for you! If none of these assumptions describe you, keep reading anyway. It's a great book, and when you finish reading it, we trust that you'll know a few things about zero trust security.

Icons Used in This Book

Throughout this book, we occasionally use special icons to call attention to important information. Here's what to expect:

REMEMBER This icon points out information you should commit to your nonvolatile memory, your gray matter, or your noggin!

TIP Tips are appreciated, never expected — and we sure hope you appreciate these useful nuggets of information.

WARNING These alerts point out the stuff your mother warned you about (well, probably not), but they do offer practical advice.

TECHNICAL STUFF If you seek to attain the seventh level of NERD-vana, perk up! This icon explains the jargon beneath the jargon.

Beyond the Book

There's only so much we can cover in 32 short pages, so if you find yourself at the end of this book thinking "where can I learn more," just go to www.edgewise.net.

IN THIS CHAPTER

» Getting past perimeter-based security

» Keeping up with application portability

» Securing cloud and dynamic environments

Chapter **1**
The Basics of Zero Trust Security

In this chapter, you explore the limitations of perimeter-based security models in the current architectural era, which necessitates new security controls for modern data center, cloud, container, and serverless environments.

Recognizing the Limitations of Traditional Network Security

The complexity of today's hybrid, multi-cloud network environments has rendered traditional perimeter-based security obsolete. Unlike the networks of old, with a clearly defined boundary (protected by a firewall) between the "trusted" (internal) network and the Internet, modern networks span on-premises data centers, as well as multiple public and private clouds, containers, serverless architectures, and virtualized environments. These heterogeneous networks are accessed not only from the corporate headquarters but also by remote workers, contractors, and partners through mobile devices.

These realities introduce new technological challenges:

- **You can't rein in the cloud with on-premises processes and controls.** Many organizations manage separate security processes and controls for their on-premises and cloud environments. This is often necessary because modern cloud workloads are elastic and, in some cases, serverless. It's often impractical to operate security policies with controls that weren't designed to dynamically scale and adapt instantaneously. For this reason, security teams are burdened with increasingly managing multiple sets of policies and controls for different network environments, requiring additional synchronization tasks and increasing maintenance overhead, complexity, costs, and risk due to potential errors.

- **Lateral movement is a cirrus problem in the cloud.** In a perimeter-based security model, users and applications "inside" the network are treated as trusted entities. Attackers use phishing, stolen credentials, or some other exploit to gain access to the internal network, piggyback on firewall policies, or abuse trust to move laterally within the network after they've slipped past the "security checkpoint."

- **Visibility is obscured by clouds.** Cloud environments are nebulous and highly dynamic with constantly moving workloads that aren't necessarily bound to traditional networking constructs like IP addresses, ports, and payloads. IP addresses are constantly changing in cloud environments, making it practically impossible to implement effective IP-based controls. In public clouds, where customers have no access to the underlying infrastructure but are still responsible for the security of the applications and data running in those environments, visibility and control can be a significant challenge. As a result, security teams are often oblivious to blind spots and vulnerabilities in the cloud.

WARNING

The lack of visibility and control in the modern network environment allows attackers to dwell inside the network for an average of over 200 days! During that time, attackers use the inherent trust given to those "inside the network" to deliver malicious payloads, establish persistence, escalate privileges, and exfiltrate valuable data.

TECHNICAL STUFF

According to the CrowdStrike *2018 Threat Report,* the average breakout time (the time it takes an attacker to move from the initial foothold to other systems in the network) in 2017 was less than two hours.

REMEMBER: The principle of least privilege requires granting only the minimum permissions necessary to perform a given task.

The zero trust security model, originally proposed by Forrester Research, shifts the perimeter-based security paradigm from "trust but verify" to "never trust, always verify." The zero trust model acknowledges the reality that the Internet is a hostile environment, and if your network connects to the Internet, then your internal network is a part of the Internet and, by extension, your network is a hostile environment — replete with both external and internal threats. Zero trust also means that security practitioners can no longer look at their networks as having an "inside" and an "outside"; some malicious traffic will never reach the external Internet but can be just as damaging.

WARNING: The 2018 Verizon *Data Breach Investigations Report* warns that insider threats — which account for 15 percent of breaches and 82 percent of all insider and privilege misuse incidents — can take months or years to detect, so obtaining user credentials is a key objective for any attacker.

Rather than assuming that the internal network is trusted because it is "inside" the perimeter, the "never trust, always verify" principle of zero trust means trust is based on the authenticated identity of every entity (application, host, container, user) and transaction and is continuously asserted.

Bringing Protection Closer to the Application Workload

Traditional port-based (or packet filtering) firewalls deployed at a network perimeter allow or block traffic between two networks or segments within a network based on source and destination IP addresses and Transmission Control Protocol (TCP) or User Datagram Protocol (UDP) port information.

REMEMBER: The vast majority of network traffic today is "east-west" (for example, server-to-server, application-to-application, and application-to-database), which is never inspected by a firewall deployed at the perimeter. After attackers slip past the firewall, it's substantially easier for them to move laterally inside the network and access critical business applications by piggybacking

CHAPTER 1 **The Basics of Zero Trust Security** 5

on approved policies and credentials. Zero trust policies on the internal network prevent lateral movement because they don't assume that the traffic is trusted because the firewall allowed the traffic onto the network at the perimeter in the first place.

This "black (block) and white (allow)" approach to network security is no longer effective because

- **Applications aren't all black and white.** Enterprises used to rely on a few core business applications, which made it relatively easy for a firewall to determine which applications should be allowed (core business applications) and which ones should be blocked (everything else). Today, enterprises seemingly use an unlimited number of critical business applications — whether sanctioned by the enterprise or not — to perform legitimate business functions. Additionally, not all applications are clearly good or bad. For example, PowerShell and Telnet are two tools commonly used by admins to perform legitimate network administration tasks. However, these "dual use" applications are also frequently used by attackers for malicious purposes.

- **Statistics don't lie; numbers do.** IP addresses and port numbers can be easily spoofed. Technically, it's about as difficult as writing someone else's return address on an envelope. In addition to spoofing, applications — both good and bad — use techniques such as port hopping, non-standard ports, tunneling, and Secure Sockets Layer (SSL) hiding to make them easier to install and run, as well as to ensure privacy and to hide their true identity, evade detection, and exfiltrate sensitive data. Attackers use these same techniques to piggyback on approved internal firewall policies (for example, IP- and port-based microsegmentation) to move laterally inside the cloud and data center.

- **Clouds (and virtual workloads) are always in motion.** In today's dynamic IT environments, IP addresses don't mean what they once did. In the not too distant past, IP addresses seldom changed. In fact, many legacy applications would actually stop working if you tried to change the IP address. And standing up a new server could take weeks or longer due to lengthy procurement cycles and cumbersome installation processes. You also had to physically carry the servers to the data center, and it was all uphill — both ways! But in today's virtual, elastic environments, new servers spin up, spin down, and move locations in minutes and seconds. Security controls that rely on constantly changing parameters such as IP addresses, port numbers, and physical locations are a policy management nightmare.

WARNING: As a result of these challenges, many IT organizations deploy overly permissive policy sets on their firewalls so they don't negatively impact business agility — but in so doing, they put their entire organization at greater risk of a security breach.

TIP: To achieve better network security by applying the zero trust principle, you need to bring protection closer to your application workloads by

- » Identifying and validating the applications communicating in your environment — on both sides of the conversation
- » Defining your security policies in terms of the secure identities of the communicating applications, independent of their IP addresses or ports
- » Deploying these policies in a dynamic environment, independent of the network infrastructure, so they can automatically adapt to rapid change — whether in a private or public cloud, a containerized or microservices application, or a staging or production environment

Reducing Risk in Cloud-based and Dynamic Architectures

Application development is integral to many businesses. Software companies aside, every retailer, bank, hospitality chain, manufacturer — you name it — is developing applications to make the customer, partner, and employee experience better, faster, and more efficient.

Development teams, for their part, are increasingly leveraging container environments to help them meet business demands for greater agility and faster time-to-market. Containers provide a fully self-contained, virtual operating system environment (OSE) that enables developers to rapidly package and deploy their applications in the cloud.

Although the containers themselves are generally designed to be secure, access to the containers themselves is not (remember, obtaining user credentials is a key objective for attackers). After an attacker gains access to a container, he can modify workloads, inject malware, delete data, uncover intellectual property, and more.

TECHNICAL STUFF

A recent report by cloud security vendor Lacework showed that the administration consoles of over 22,000 container orchestration and application programming interface (API) management systems were exposed to the Internet. Vulnerable systems include Docker, Kubernetes, OpenShift, and others. While most of the container orchestration tools require credentials to access the internal environment, the consoles themselves expose organization- and function-specific information that could potentially be used by an attacker. The Lacework report also found that more than 300 companies hadn't properly configured the container administration tools to require login credentials for access. Additional compensating security controls, like firewalls or virtual private network (VPN) access, were also absent.

Unfortunately, this theme is common with the deployment of cloud-based tools and services. Though most cloud providers offer various security controls, a significant portion of those controls are based on IP addresses, ports, and protocols, which can be circumvented by wily attackers.

REMEMBER

Organizations need to stop trusting network constructs and instead focus on protecting applications, workloads, and data — their core assets — communicating in the cloud, by verifying the identities of the communicating entities that are accessing the data, rather than the environment itself. Moving protection directly to the workload and implementing zero trust is the best way to ensure attackers can't tamper with them.

> **IN THIS CHAPTER**
> » Moving to a zero trust security strategy
> » Knowing what you're protecting
> » Gaining visibility and control of "east-west" traffic
> » Starting with no trust and building up
> » Simplifying and automating your security policies

Chapter 2
Implementing an Inside-Out Methodology

In this chapter, we explain the zero trust methodology and how to apply it to your organization's strategic assets.

Understanding the Methodology

When asked why he robbed banks, the notorious American bank robber Willie Sutton is reputed to have answered "Because that's where the money is" (though he denied having ever said this). Today, cybercriminals rob data centers because that's where the money (data) is. But unlike a traditional bank robber, cybercriminals don't need to worry about breaking into a secure vault inside the bank or evading countermeasures such as security cameras, silent alarms, and dye packs. After they slip past the "security guard" (firewall) at the front door, valuables are readily accessible.

The "bank" is open 24 hours a day, 7 days a week, and getting past the security guard is a matter of answering three questions:

» Where are you from (source IP address)?
» Where are you going (destination IP address)?
» What are you doing (pick a port number between 1 and 65,536 to describe yourself)?

As long as you aren't on the list of blocked source addresses, destination addresses, or applications, you're in! And if you are on the list, just change your answer — no one's verifying your answers anyway. Or you can just follow a trusted bank employee into the building (by using compromised credentials).

It's unlikely that you would do business with a bank that relied only on perimeter-based security to keep your money safe. You expect to see armed security guards, alarm panels, security cameras, and a locked vault when you walk into your bank. And when you make a cash withdrawal, you expect the bank teller to positively identify you by requiring you to produce a photo ID every time you want to make a withdrawal. In other words, your bank has zero trust that you are who you say you are until you pass all its security checks, every time you visit your bank — and you welcome this level of scrutiny because it's your money they're protecting.

Similarly, zero trust shifts the cybersecurity focus away from traditional perimeter defense as the primary method of attack prevention and toward securing the assets (systems and applications) that contain the data and information that needs to be protected. It's an "inside-out" approach that protects your strategic assets as close to the asset as possible and trusts no one or thing — even if it's an application inside the data center — until it has been properly vetted against established policies.

Mapping Your Attack Surface

A fundamental element of zero trust is understanding what key assets (systems, applications, and data) your organization has so that appropriate protections can be built around them, as close to the asset as is possible. Okay, we're talking about identifying and classifying your assets, but because "inventory your assets" doesn't sound cool, you need to "map your attack surface." After all, your assets — including how those assets communicate (data flows) — comprise your attack surface.

To protect their systems, applications, and data, organizations must first know what they are, where they are, and how they travel through the network. Identifying these key assets allows the organization to take a data-first, inside-out approach, which is necessary because everything touches the data: applications, systems, networks, devices, and users. Therefore, every organization needs to know what assets they have and how those assets interact with each other on the network. This knowledge is particularly important in today's increasingly hybrid, multi-cloud environments where an organization doesn't always know (but should) how its data gets from Point A to Point B.

TIP Identifying the organization's key assets improves visibility (because today most organizations don't maintain a complete and up-to-date asset inventory), increases data awareness, and enables the implementation of a zero trust strategy.

Preventing Lateral Movement by Attackers

The key to initiating a successful cyberattack against a targeted organization is to first gain access to the environment. In a somewhat similar manner as the principle of least privilege, attackers will often initially target the "least common denominator" or the weakest link in an organization — which is often the organization's end-users and their devices.

The reason that gaining access is so important is that once attackers access a traditional network that relies on perimeter-based security, they're free to roam the network — like a bank without a vault.

TECHNICAL STUFF According to the CrowdStrike *2018 Threat Report*, the "average breakout time [the time it takes an attacker to move from the initial entry point to other targets on the network] in 2017 was only one hour and 58 minutes." After an attacker has successfully infiltrated a network, the average dwell time is 99 days according to a 2018 FireEye threat report. A recent Edgewise report also found that network overexposure within the perimeter is greater than 95 percent in most organizations, which, given that an average of 19 Common Vulnerabilities and Exposures (CVEs) are published daily and the average time to fix a CVE-identified vulnerability is 50 days, creates an unacceptably large window of opportunity for attackers.

The combination of excessive dwell time and network overexposure, shown in Figure 2-1, creates an ideal environment for attackers to move laterally and wreak havoc in the network.

TIME + EXPOSURE = LATERAL MOVEMENT

99 DAYS DWELL TIME (global median) — TIME

\>95% NETWORK OVEREXPOSURE (within perimeter)

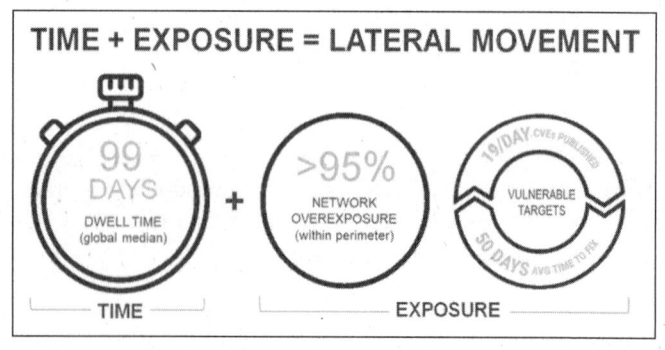

19/DAY CVEs PUBLISHED
VULNERABLE TARGETS
50 DAYS AVG TIME TO FIX

— EXPOSURE —

FIGURE 2-1: Lateral movement by attackers.

Traditional security designs, such as firewalls deployed at the perimeter, only inspect and allow or block "north-south" traffic — traffic that traverses the firewall going to or from a "trusted" zone (such as the enterprise network) to an "untrusted" zone (such as the Internet).

The problem with these traditional security designs is that as much as 80 percent of all network traffic today is "east-west" traffic between servers, applications, and devices on the network, in the data center, or in the cloud — traffic that potentially never traverses a firewall and is therefore never inspected. It is in this free-spirited environment that adversaries thrive.

REMEMBER

Preventing lateral movement by attackers is critical to stopping a cyberattack in its tracks. Zero trust security accomplishes this by moving protection as close as possible to your strategic assets — systems, applications, and data — so every asset, in effect, has its own security perimeter that never trusts and always verifies.

Implementing Least Privilege

The principle of least privilege is a well understood, if not fully implemented, maxim in information security. A user or "thing" (such as an application or service) should only have the minimum permissions required to perform a given (authorized) function.

The problem with most tools' implementations is that they typically begin by granting access to everything, and then they selectively remove permissions until just before the point that the user or thing can no longer perform the required task. With group-based permissions and "one-off" situations proliferating, "privilege creep" becomes a real problem.

Instead, zero trust begins with an absolute, literal interpretation of "least privilege" — that is, *no* privilege! Never trust, always verify means that you begin with no permissions and selectively add permissions, only up to the point that a user or thing can perform a given (authorized) function.

But zero trust doesn't end with never trust. The second part of the zero trust philosophy, "always verify," means that "just because I trusted you last month, last week, or five minutes ago doesn't mean I trust you now." A zero trust strategy requires continuous identification, verification, and monitoring.

REMEMBER Zero trust doesn't mean you never attest trust. It means you stop assuming trust based on locations (relative to the "perimeter") and addresses, and instead, you continuously assert the minimum level of trust necessary based on the verified identities of the entities and transactions themselves.

Creating Application Workload Centric Policies for Cloud Agility

Many businesses unfortunately perceive security as a business inhibitor that creates bottlenecks and stifles innovation and agility. But in much the same way that brakes on a car don't make the car go slower, they allow it to go faster (how fast would you go if you couldn't stop?), a zero trust strategy is a business enabler that allows the business to securely leverage the agility and scale of the cloud, containers, as well as other innovative new technologies, such as Internet of Things (IoT) implementations. While at first glance starting with "never trust" seems like it would increase friction within an organization, zero trust actually decreases complexity for the organization by improving visibility (provided you've identified your strategic assets, both on-premises and in the cloud) and creating a control plane that's portable (because it centers on the asset, not the network in which the asset runs).

This means security teams can implement and automate a standard set of policies that can be applied uniformly at the application workload level across on-premises, hybrid, and multi-cloud environments — no more trying to retrofit outmoded controls to modern environments (that is, clouds and containers) or attempting to maintain disparate sets of policies across different toolsets and environments. Zero trust is a holistic and standardized approach to security that leads to better visibility, which, in turn, reduces risk throughout the enterprise.

IN THIS CHAPTER

» Looking at risk

» Creating a digital fingerprint

» Extracting the "DNA" of your application workloads

Chapter **3**

Verifying Application Workload Identities

In this chapter, we explain how to understand and visualize risk in your environment and the importance of fingerprinting and positively identifying your application workloads.

Understanding and Visualizing Risk

Up to 98 percent of network pathways in an organization's cloud or data center environment aren't required for application workloads to perform their normal function. Attackers exploit these pathways to move laterally through the environment toward their ultimate targets, such as databases containing customer records. It's therefore crucial to identify and visualize these pathways (data flows) to fully understand workload risk in your environment:

» **Reveal risk for specific applications or hosts.** Verify the secure identity ("fingerprint") of communicating workloads using the zero trust model and filter applications or hosts of interest to assess their exposure.

» **Review overall (over)exposure of applications or hosts in your environment.** Quantify network paths beyond those necessary for business services to perform their business function. Understand how many application communication pathways are currently protected, could be protected with available policies, or have no protection policies available.

» **Evaluate exposure of specific applications or hosts in your environment to prioritize remediation.** Identify network pathways that aren't necessary for the business application or host to communicate and eliminate these potential attack vectors. Quantify the pathways that can be protected with zero trust policies that allow only verified applications, users, and hosts to communicate.

Fingerprinting Workloads

As we discuss in Chapters 1 and 2, identifying applications by arbitrary IP addresses and port numbers is futile in the modern application and threat landscape. Instead, application workloads and services need to be identified by their attributes, characteristics, and other immutable properties to allow security teams to implement effective policies based on which applications and data are present and communicating on the network. Doing so decouples security policy from the underlying network infrastructure (and changes to it) and ties it directly to the strategic assets that are being protected.

Application identity has four keys, which are covered in this section.

Unchanging characteristics

An application's identity must be based on immutable properties that an attacker can't change (for example, version and product name, digital certificate, loaded modules, command line arguments, and file location) and a cryptographic hash of a binary file of the application (for example, the Secure Hash Algorithm, or SHA256). If a single bit of the binary file changes, the hash will result in a different value, and you'll get a different identity.

Examples of unchanging characteristics in a system include attributes like the universally unique identifier (UUID) of the system's basic input/output system (BIOS) and serial numbers of the processors — things that are so fundamental to the system that an attacker can't change them.

Immutability ensures that the core characteristics of an application or service remain reliable enough to uniquely identify each application or service for verification in a zero trust environment while continuing to allow the application or service to be upgraded, updated, or improved, when necessary (and authorized).

REMEMBER Zero trust security policies based on application fingerprints must be immutable so they can't be tampered with, but they must be flexible enough to allow applications to be upgraded or updated without requiring the entire policy to be rewritten.

Understandable characteristics

One problem with using traditional security tools to protect applications on the network is translating "application speak" (how the application was designed to communicate) into "network speak" (how security policies are written). This "failure to communicate" causes much frustration and angst between development and security teams and results in inadequate protections for critical workloads.

To avoid this internal conflict, using understandable characteristics of applications and their intended communication paths to define policies means that security and networking and development and application teams can communicate using a common language. Oblique, opaque, or arbitrary characteristics erode confidence in the usefulness of traditional network constructs as identifiers. Using characteristics that make sense to the practitioner makes practitioners more likely to trust and use the resulting application identity.

A broad variety of characteristics

An application's identity must be based on a combination of many attributes, not just a smattering that could potentially be used to identify multiple applications. Identifying an application based on a large collection of attributes means that some parts of the identity can change (for example, due to software updates) without changing the overall fingerprint of the application.

Using a cross section of attributes provides the baseline for the application's identity and allows administrators to add other, more variable traits that further describe the application, without losing confidence in the accuracy and viability of the identity.

By using a broad variety of characteristics, organizations can choose the ones that comprise the correct combination of features, which allows them to make the best generalizations about the identity and behavior of the application when it's communicating on the network. In a practical zero trust implementation, this process is automated and leverages machine learning to select the attributes that most reliably identify the applications, with provisions for humans to check, verify, and see what attributes are being used by the system.

Upgrade tolerant

Application fingerprints must be upgrade tolerant, allowing for new versions of software without necessitating an overhaul of security policies every time software is patched or upgraded.

Verifying Identity

Computer networking has traditionally relied on "unique" identifiers — namely, IP addresses, port numbers, and protocols — to verify that a user, system, traffic, or application is what it says it is. In other words, "my identity is my identity; therefore, I am who I say I am." This approach, however, is very simplistic and assumes that no two entities can have the same identity, or that no user, system, traffic, or application can spoof another's identity. In today's not-so-simplistic world of networking, most technologies haven't moved past this notion of an IP address as a verifier, and cybercriminals have evolved their tools and techniques to take advantage of this false notion.

Better ways to verify identity do exist by taking a lesson out of the playbooks of newer technologies. Consider, for example, the recent uptick in caller ID spoofing. Odds are you've gotten dozens of phone calls on your personal cellphone that appear to be coming from not just your area code, but also an identical prefix as your own number. The idea is that you're more likely to answer a call that appears to come from a neighbor, and those who have phone numbers very similar to yours are more likely to be your neighbors.

But as we all know, those calls aren't actually coming from your neighbors; they're being faked to entice you to answer when your phone rings.

In contrast, think of all the ways in which you need to identify and verify yourself when calling your doctor's office or credit card company today. Simply stating your name and confirming your home address (which can generally be found online) isn't enough. These providers require answers to additional questions, such as "What's your secret passphrase, account number, and date of last transaction/appointment?" This multi-factor process of verifying identity means that threat actors are less likely to be able to spoof an identity.

With respect to identifying and securing business applications and software built for enterprise use, security and networking teams continue to try to force outdated constructs onto development team workflows. Developers are, to put it bluntly, not thinking about IP addresses and firewall rules. Security is speaking a different language, and it's one that doesn't conform to how software is written and deployed today.

The fact is, the failure to effectively translate "application speak" to "network speak" poses serious threats to enterprises, and the technologies security teams are using to try to mitigate those threats simply aren't adequate. A dynamic application communication topology and data paths can't be effectively modeled through traditional network or address constructs to implement least privilege control and protection. Firewalls — one of the main security technologies implemented to deal with identifying and verifying traffic — rely on IP addresses, ports, and some aspects of the application protocol to detect those threats. It's impossible for firewalls to define policies with true application identities at the core because looking at IP addresses, protocols, and packets isn't enough. At the end of the day, the goal is to stop malicious actions.

However, inferring identity and intent from a few numbers in a network packet is next to impossible, but adding detailed insight regarding each of the communicating applications makes the job not only possible, but feasible.

REMEMBER

Verifying identity with zero trust means that each and every time a communication on the network is requested, the fingerprint of the system and workload must be examined and validated by using cryptographic properties and an aggregation of immutable attributes, such as loaded modules, command line

CHAPTER 3 **Verifying Application Workload Identities** 19

arguments, software versions, product names, and so on. This pre-connect validation ensures that a spoofed ID or maliciously-altered software can't propagate throughout the network and cause a compromise or breach. Taking it up one level, applying a zero trust methodology means *not* assuming that just because a user, host, application, or workload was verified and deemed "trusted" once — based on properties that can be faked, guessed, or stolen — that it should still be trusted. In true zero trust form, never trust, always verify application workload identities.

> **IN THIS CHAPTER**
> » Knowing what you're protecting
> » Building a map of your data flows
> » Creating security rules and policies
> » Continuously evolving your strategy through automation

Chapter 4
Getting Started with Zero Trust Security

Zero trust security has become a guiding architectural principle (if not implemented as such, it's at least a worthy goal) for security-conscious organizations today. In this chapter, we lay out four steps that you can take to implement zero trust security in your organization.

Step 1: Identify Your Assets

Before you can deploy appropriate security protections anywhere on your network, it's crucial to know what exactly it is that you're protecting. The first step to implementing zero trust security is to inventory (or map your attack surface, if you will) the applications, workloads, and data stores that are communicating in your cloud and data center environment.

After you've completed your inventory (which should be automated to ensure it's always up to date), consider classifying assets by risk, sensitivity, and exposure to compromise. This process allows you to identify high-profile assets and appropriately prioritize their protection.

TIP: Take an inventory of your users, employee devices, corporate systems, applications, and workloads:

- » Internal systems are as important as remote users.
- » Consider classifying assets by risk, sensitivity, and exposure.
- » Don't "boil the ocean."

TIP: Start with your most valuable assets first (for example, core databases that contain customer data, payment information, health care records, and so on).

Step 2: Analyze Your Data Flows

After you know what you need to protect, the next step is to understand how those assets are communicating across the network, what they're accessing, and how. Before you start to map data flows, get your application stakeholders (that is, your IT and business colleagues) involved to understand what applications they use and how they're using them. When undertaking the mapping process, it's important to take workflows into account so that accurate baselines can be established. This process should be automated to ensure the information is always up to date (manual flow diagrams are outdated as quickly as they are created).

TIP: Analyze your network. How are applications and services communicating across your network? What data stores are being accessed? Is there a business need for a database containing all the customer records to be accessed by an application? Is dual-use software (for example, PowerShell) being used? How is that controlled?

Step 3: Protect Strategic Assets

After identifying and analyzing your environment, it's time to apply appropriate protections to your assets — as close to the asset as possible — with baseline policies that enforce least-privilege access based on required data flows. The rules for policies should take into account users, devices, workloads, and the intended targets of attackers. Verification of whether these assets are allowed to connect must be based on multiple data sources (instead of the IP addresses or ports from which they originate).

This is known as *application* or *workload identity* and is another core tenet of zero trust (see Chapter 3).

TIP: Accomplishing this step requires the use of entity-aware tools that analyze asset identity (or fingerprint) as the means by which something is allowed or denied.

REMEMBER: Apply protection with baseline policies that enforce minimum access based on required data flows:

» Create rules based on the identity of devices, users, workloads, and targets (data stores).

» Base trust on as many immutable attributes of the workload as possible.

» Use tools that have true visibility into applications that are communicating (not network address-based tools, such as firewalls).

Step 4: Monitor and Adapt

No strategy or tool can be effective indefinitely without changing or adapting to a continuously evolving threat landscape. Zero trust is no exception. Therefore, after you've inventoried your environment, mapped data flows, and implemented appropriate security policies for the assets that you're trying to protect, the crux of success lies in your ability to continuously monitor your environment and tune your strategy and tools as needed. Also, don't underestimate the importance of monitoring internal (east-west) traffic.

TIP: Zero trust networking is most effective when the process and policies are automated and can easily adapt to change. Security doesn't have to impede agility, and basing your security strategy on a zero trust methodology allows you to move from "trusted" networks with insecure workloads to networks that continuously verify workloads, even if the environment is inherently insecure.

REMEMBER: Continuously monitor application flows and adjust as needed, and remember the following:

» Internal (east-west) traffic is as important (if not more so) than external (north-south) traffic.

CHAPTER 4 **Getting Started with Zero Trust Security** 23

>> Zero trust networking is most effective when the process is automated, and policies readily adapt to change.

USING AUTOMATION TO PROTECT CLOUD WORKLOADS

When it comes to the cloud, many companies aren't entirely sure how to use automation outside their on-premises environment, or how or where cloud workload protection fits into their technology stack. Plenty of traditional security automation tools exist, but they don't necessarily adapt well to highly dynamic environments. When a company operates in a hybrid cloud environment, managing multiple sets of tools — one for the cloud and another for the internal data center — adds maintenance overhead, which is costly and inefficient.

If the organization is unaware of the presence of software, services, or even entire workloads, there is little to no chance of securing them. Rapid development and deployment cycles result in the need for ongoing automation to rapidly and effectively apply security. Because new deployments and changes, themselves, are continuous, visibility must be too. Automation provides the real-time visibility that enables

- Fast and accurate asset discovery and elimination of network "blind spots"
- Quicker incident and issue response
- Accelerated decision making
- Visualization of security risks across environments

Automating asset discovery and change in the cloud is one of the best ways security can stay on top of what's present in the cloud and what needs to be protected.

Using an automated cloud workload protection tool that will scale across both on-premises and multi-cloud environments significantly reduces security complexity and means the organization can maintain one set of security policies that travel with the workload, wherever it's running. Policy management, which is often a huge nightmare for IT and security teams using traditional tools, becomes streamlined, allowing for easier administration and faster response times.

> **IN THIS CHAPTER**
> - » Decreasing risk and gaining greater control
> - » Lowering breach potential and aiding compliance efforts
> - » Increasing business speed and agility and reducing organizational friction

Chapter **5**

The Business Benefits of Zero Trust Security

In this chapter, we outline the business benefits of moving to a zero trust model.

Reduce Risk by Identifying Assets and Improving Visibility

One major blind spot for many organizations is knowing precisely what data they have, where it resides, and how it's being accessed. After all, how can you secure it if you don't know it exists? With the proliferation of mobile devices, the Internet of Things (IoT), and rapid and continuous deployment of new applications and services, IT and security teams are hard pressed to achieve 100 percent visibility (when using traditional address-based tools and techniques) on every data packet that traverses the network. With zero trust, however, any applications or services that attempt to communicate inside the network are first identified, then assumed inherently untrustworthy, and automatically disallowed from communication unless their identity fingerprint is verified. In this way, security, IT, and networking teams can use zero trust to understand what's already on the network and what's trying to get there.

Further, because data flows are mapped, a zero trust network provides better visibility into the network and associated risks.

Gain Greater Control in Your Cloud Environment

Security practitioners' biggest and longest-held fears of moving to and using the cloud are loss of visibility and lack of control. Despite the evolution in cloud service providers' (CSP) security due diligence, workload security remains a shared responsibility between the CSP and the organization using the cloud. That said, there's only so much the organization can affect inside someone else's cloud.

REMEMBER Zero trust is tailor-made for any type of network — including public and hybrid clouds. A zero trust network protects communication by allowing only workloads verified by their identity fingerprint to communicate. Because zero trust is application workload centric (rather than perimeter or network centric), security teams have greater control over the application workload itself. Any time a workload fails to meet attribute recognition, it isn't allowed to communicate, which means attackers have a much harder time achieving east-west lateral movement — movement that's hard to detect and protect against in traditional, perimeter-based network environments.

Achieve Lower Breach Potential

Because the zero trust model is focused on the workload, it's easier for security teams to identify and stop malicious activity. A zero trust network continuously inspects workload communication patterns for deviations from the intended state and prevents workloads that are unverified from communicating with malicious command and control (C&C) infrastructure or anywhere else on the network (between hosts, users, or applications — and any combination thereof). Any altered application or service, whether it's a result of malicious activity, misuse, or accident, is automatically untrusted until it can be verified again through a set of policies and controls (which may be automated or manual, depending on the tools in use). Additionally, even when verified and approved, communication is restricted to a need-to-know basis, (that is, access is locked down to only the users, hosts, or services that require access — also known as the principle of least privilege).

This inherent distrust results in decreased breach potential and therefore decreased risk, not to mention fewer cleanup and mitigation costs (because there are fewer breaches).

Aid Compliance Audit Initiatives

Every security professional understands that compliance doesn't equal security, but that doesn't eliminate the compliance burden. Auditors have the ear of executive teams, if for no other reason than that failed audits can lead to business disruptions and negative financial impact. Security teams, therefore, must play nicely in the audit sandbox.

Auditors aren't meant to be the playground tattletale, but the reality is that IT audits, in particular, are focused on highlighting technology weaknesses. This means that any problems with data access or the systems that maintain them are subject to scrutiny. Anything security teams can do to shore up weaknesses before an audit occurs not only smooths the audit process but also ratchets up protection.

REMEMBER

With zero trust in place, auditors (and others in the organization) achieve clearer insight into how applications are communicating and accessing key data stores in a protected manner, with the principle of least privilege access firmly in place. Zero trust mitigates the number of places and ways network communications can be exploited, and results in fewer negative audit findings and less remediation for the security team.

Increase Business Speed and Agility

Today's businesses strive to operate at lightning speed, and address-, protocol-, and port-based security controls can run contrary to those efforts. Whenever a port is blocked or a host is shut down because of a possible intrusion, for instance, employees can't access the data or services required to do their jobs. When a breach occurs, multiple disruptions accompany it. If the development team goes to deploy an application and security says, "No, stop. That's insecure," release is halted (and frustrations flare).

The ability to move continually forward and pivot on a dime is a highly-coveted business goal, and a zero trust network allows that to happen because it works seamlessly in the background. Protection travels alongside the workload rather than at a far-off security "checkpoint," meaning that any blocked or disallowed communication is isolated and no interruptions to speed and agility exist. In other words, in a zero trust network, security isn't constrained by static network constructs that slow it down.

Alleviate Organizational Friction

Software and applications dominate business, and DevOps has paved the pathway for today's rapid development initiatives. The advent of containers and other dynamic, distributed development and staging environments has allowed DevOps teams to work even more efficiently but has introduced increased numbers of vulnerabilities, which are nearly impossible for security teams to manage with traditional controls.

In the past, security either tried to nose its way into the DevOps process or bolted protections onto already-deployed software, neither of which worked well. The problem with both approaches is translating application "speak" into network "speak"; too much manual intervention is required and slows down what's meant to be an accelerated process.

REMEMBER

Zero trust knocks out these issues by effectively enveloping applications in protection. As applications are deployed, they're assigned an identity fingerprint. Provided that fingerprint remains the same or matches that of an already-verified application, it's allowed to communicate freely. Changes or updates to the application don't necessarily change the fingerprint — in the same way that a new suit or visit to a new city doesn't alter a person's identity — which means that DevOps can conduct business as usual and not have to worry about security raining on their parade. In the sense that software and services create business opportunities, any approach security can adopt (such as zero trust) that tames tensions and aligns with business priorities — while introducing greater protection — is a win.